CW00853511

For Isabella and Sophie
xxxx

Barbara Bingers Has Carrots For Fingers

Written and Illustrated by
Janek Puzon

In a little house, at the end of the
street,
Lived a unique girl that you're about
to meet.

Barbara Bingers was her name,
But like you and I, she was not the
same.

You see, Barbara had a special gift,
Something different, if you catch my drift.

I won't allow the uncertainty to linger,
But Barbara Bingers had carrots for fingers!

She got up one morning and thought she'd like,
To go outside and ride on her bike.

But because she had carrots for fingers instead,
She fell off her bike and then bumped her head!

Her friends would ask her to go to the park,
To play and have fun before it got dark.

But for Barbara, it wasn't a pleasant sight,
Her carrot fingers fumbling to hold her kite!

Barbara went to the beach when her friends
asked her to come,
But she'd be bored and sit looking glum.

It honestly wasn't worth the hassle,
Carrot fingers weren't ideal to build a
sandcastle!

In the winter, when it would snow,
When the temperature reached minus two below.

Barbara would get her mum to knit,
Special mittens that would hopefully fit.

Making snowballs and snowmen was very tough,
After ten minutes of trying, Barbara had had
enough.

And for a joke, her friends would ask her to place,
A finger for a nose on the snowman's face!

Playing catch, waxing cars, tying a shoe,
All things that Barbara struggled to do.

It was a nightmare when putting on clothes,
And even harder when picking her nose!

But then came a day that you wouldn't expect,
A day you couldn't predict, I do suspect.

Farmer Trent had put out a plea,
That shocked the town, I guarantee.

MISSING!!!!

Jeff the donkey.
Beloved pet of Farmer Trent.
Last seen playing football with the
LADS.

Likes   Dislikes
● Long walks   ● Smelly wellies
● Carrots   ● Cliff edges
● Game shows   ● Horror films

If you see him, please contact Farmer Trent down at the farm

His donkey, Jeff, had gone for a wander,
Up high in the mountains and over yonder.

Jeff, unbelievably, was frozen stiff,
As he perched on the edge of a dangerous cliff!

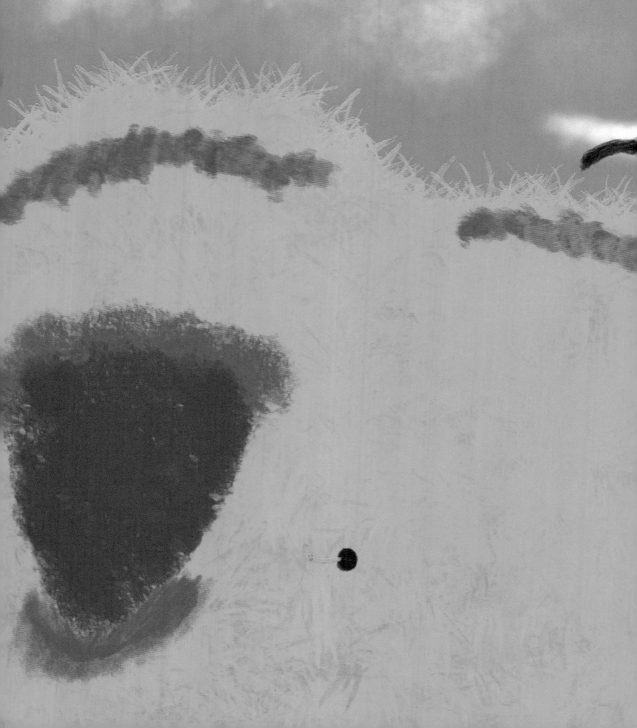

The town then thought of what they could do,
But Barbara's friends believed that they knew.

They could use the help of Barbara's hands,
To bring Jeff back down to less dangerous land.

So a fire engine set off and headed towards,
The bottom of the cliff with Barbara on board!

On a ladder, she was raised
up and moved to the mound,

Waving her carrot fingers to
the crowds on the ground!

At first, Jeff was reluctant to move,
He was scared and wouldn't budge his hooves.

But then the smell of Barbara's fists,
Was the greatest thing to ever exist!

Jeff then hopped onto the ladder,
showing no fear,

As the watching crowd all started to
cheer!

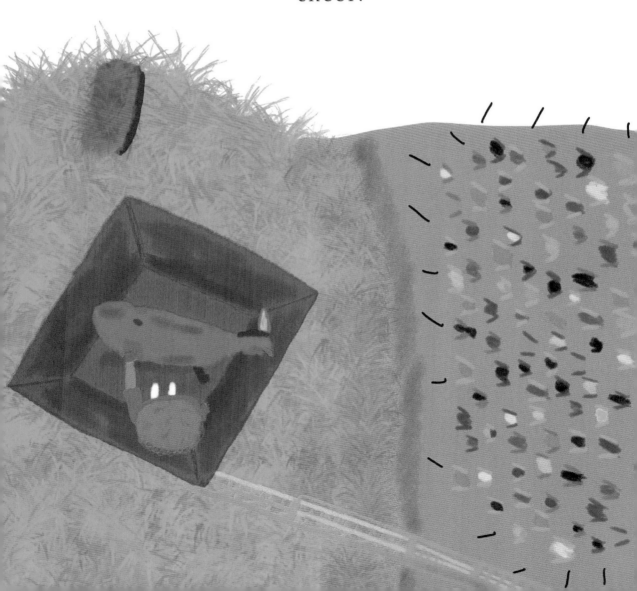

From being scared and going through the
wringer,
Jeff was now licking Barbara's fingers!

Barbara was now a hero and had saved
the day,
The town all proud of her courageous
display.

She'd rescued the donkey, straight from the
cliff edge,
With her unusual hands that were made out
of veg!

THE
END!!

Author's (and Illustrator's) Note

I am thrilled to have provided the illustrations that accompany the words I've written for this book. Not as thrilled as I was when I first discovered peanut butter brownies, but it's a close second.

I worked overtime in ensuring the book was of good quality, that it was available for the general public to read as soon as possible and also because I couldn't handle any more 'is it ready yet?' questions from my two children.

Finally, a shout out to Mrs Radford, the art teacher at Darwen Vale school, who helped to create a megastar with a pencil. I knew all of those classes would come in handy for drawing a girl with carrot fingers, 30 years later.

<u>Acknowledgements</u>

I'd like to thank my wife and children for their assistance in putting together this book. Their love and support has been greatly appreciated and enabled me to come up with the ideas for the story.

XXXX

Printed in Great Britain
by Amazon

37298122R00018